COVID, Isolation & Hope

Artists Respond to the Pandemic

edited by

Rafael Alvarado, Consuelo G. Flores and Richard Modiano

Finishing Line Press
Georgetown, Kentucky

Featuring poetry and artwork by

Rafael Alvarado * Elaine Barnard * Luis Cuauhtémoc Berriozábal

Celia Bland * Jennifer Bradpiece * Lynne Bronstein

Ranney Campbell * Marne Carmean * Eileen Carol

Patricia Carragon * Neeli Cherkovski * John Dorsey

Kim Dower * Carolina Rivera Escamilla * Consuelo G. Flores

Amélie Frank * Tammy Melody Gomez * Rachael Ikins

Victor Infante * Erika Jahneke * Eleanor Kedney

Genevieve Legacy * Aqueila M. Lewis-Ross * Peter Marti

Jim McDonald * Richard Modiano * Viggo Mortensen

Kendall Nelson * Marisela Norte * Suzanne O'Connell

Marc Olmsted * Suzi Kaplan Olmsted * Connie Owens Patton

Heather Pease * Wang Ping * Kate Robinson

Paula Rudnick * Norman Savage * Bryan Scheideck

Mark States * Laura Thurlow * George Wallace

Julene T. Weaver * Kurt Wit * Marc Zegans

COVID, Isolation & Hope

Artists Respond to the Pandemic

Copyright © 2022 Rafael Alvarado, Consuelo G. Flores and Richard Modiano
ISBN 978-1-64662-770-7 First Edition
All rights reserved under International and Pan-American Copyright Conventions.
No part of this book may be reproduced in any manner whatsoever without written
permission from the publisher, except in the case of brief quotations embodied in
critical articles and reviews.

Publisher: Leah Huete de Maines
FLP Editor: Christen Kincaid
Cover Art: "Aquis estoy Mi Amore" by Marisela Norte
Cover Design: Elizabeth Maines McCleavy

Order online: www.finishinglinepress.com
also available on amazon.com

Author inquiries and mail orders:
Finishing Line Press
P. O. Box 1626
Georgetown, Kentucky 40324
U. S. A.

Table of Contents

Hypochondriac's Dream Comes True by Kim Dower 1
the trapper & the furrier (inspired by Regina Spektor)
    by Patricia Carragon 2
CORONAVIRUS 1, HUMANS 0 by Paula Rudnick 3
Congested by Ranney Campbell 4
The Need is Greed is Want is More by Peter Marti 5
OP EN   A   LL N IGH T by Norman Savage 7
A Doctor Watching Sunset with His 87-year-old Patient in Wuhan
    by Wang Ping 9
A Litter of Supplies by Kurt Wit 12
Bless You Brother by Marc Olmsted 13
Trumpenvolk by Richard Modiano 14
Different Kind of Dinner by Tammy Melody Gomez 15
Day 9 of Self-Isolation by Kim Dower 16
Thoughts After Sitting in Daniel Crocker's Basement by John Dorsey 17
the ambulances are screaming down 7th avenue again
    by George Wallace 18
I finally found a chicken by Kim Dower 20
The Coming Darkness by Luis Cuauhtémoc Berriozábal 21
Untitled Photograph by Bryan Scheideck 22
Off the Dead by Tammy Melody Gomez 23
At a Time Like This by Julene Tripp Weaver 24
The Virus by Jennifer Bradpiece 25
Nothing is Happening by Genevieve Legacy 27
COVID POEM #2 by Suzi Kaplan-Olmsted 29
INMATES by Celia Bland 30
Poetry on the edge of the apocalypse by Victor Infante 31
A middling tide by Kate Robinson 32
Untitled Photograph by Brian Scheideck 33
Lessons Learned During a Pandemic by Connie Owens Patton 34

spring happened without men in it by George Wallace	35
crema-oratory by Marc Olmsted	36
Eudaimonia by Viggo Mortensen	37
La Escencial Photograph by Marisela Norte	43
Doing Nothing by Luis Cuauhtémoc Berriozabal	44
Just touched by Tammy Melody Gomez	45
Self-Isolating Dog by Kim Dower	46
Siren Song for Jacksonville by Eileen Carole	47
Being, Human by Heather Pease	48
Take Your Medicine this Time so You'll Know What to Do Next Time! by Aqueila M. Lewis-Ross	50
Touchless Sonnet by Lynne Bronstein	52
Hibernate by Laura Thurlow	53
Wash Your Hoofs Photograph by Rachel Ikins	55
65 Bucks by Luis Cuauhtémoc Berriozabal	56
This Is for the Birds! (for Arroe Collins) by Mark States	58
malachite, gemstone too heavy to bear by George Wallace	59
The Smarmy Thorn Must Die by Marc Zegans	61
Pandemic by Carolina Rivera Escamilla	63
Cthonic? Could Be a Cough by Amélie Frank	67
strange blues on my phantom by Marc Olmsted	69
Scooters Photograph by Jim McDonald	70
A few moments in the time of Corona March 17 2020 by Rafael Alvarado	71
blue cat at dawn by George Wallace	73
The Body Snatcher by Marc Olmsted	75
Untitled by Eleanor Kedney	76
Immersive Theater by Tammy Melody Gomez	78
Aqui Estoy Mi Amor Photograph by Marisela Norte	79
What Gives Hope by Julene Tripp Weaver	80
FOR THE WORLD DEAD by Neeli Cherkovsky	81
Untitled Photograph by Consuelo Flores	83

Introduction

2020 was an historic year. 2020 was a challenging year. 2020 was a pandemic year. 2020 was a deadly year. 2020 was.

This collection of work, which represents artists in different media and are of diverse backgrounds from throughout the United States and across the globe, have one thing in common—they all found creative ways to respond to the isolation caused by Covid-19, the virus that created the pandemic. The anthology started as a recognition by the editors that artists were using their creativity to not only document the impact of this historic, global pandemic but also their own experiences—make sense out of them, process their grief, stay connected, find closure, and ultimately embrace the possibility of hope.

The call for response work was put out through various social media platforms, direct emails and through literary centers in March 2020. We received hundreds of terrific submissions, then we created a schedule. The editors met on a weekly basis starting in Fall of 2020 to review each piece. We adhered to the guidelines we established, focusing on how each piece represented the reality of the pandemic.

It was an interesting, engaging, heartfelt and important process for the editors. In the selected work you'll find different perspectives and approaches to what the world experienced. Some is humorous, some is heartbreaking. Some is about isolation, some about connecting in a new way. Some work is about loss, some is about hope.

While the pandemic was limiting in many ways, it also opened new, unexpected doors of opportunity. The editors recognized that Covid-19, like other major events, helped many people realize how vital human connection is and how artists, despite their own challenges, found aesthetic ways to create community, create art, create life and ultimately offer an optimistic view of the future.

From the images, to the prose, to the poetry, this collection of work is inspired by the challenge of a virus that could not quell the spirit of an artist.

We hope you enjoy the work as much as we did.

Even with your mask
You are beautiful.

Marne Carmean
04-30-2020

Hypochondriac's Dream Comes True
by Kim Dower

Oh, my God, at last. A pandemic.
The word alone—pan-dem-ic, tastes so good,
the way dem bounces off the roof of my mouth,
trips from my coated tongue to my trusting lips,
a ballet of syllables dead-ending
at the back of my expectorant throat,
Coronavirus sounds like a symphony,
a beer, a place I could go in a mini-van,
if I wasn't afraid to leave my house,
knowing even washing my hands
won't be enough to protect me,
urgent call for Pandemic Preparedness
ignites me, I'm relieved this thing is real—
From this day forward, when I have a chill,
a cough, an ache, people will be forced
to take me seriously, not like when I ran
to the doctor, splinter in my toe, convinced
I had sepsis, red streaks spreading up my leg,
my foot would absolutely need to be chopped off!
I can rest knowing everyone in the world
is frightened, scared to touch their faces, shake
hands, inhale, and I will emerge triumphant,
knowing I was right to worry all these years,
since the day they lowered me into a bathtub
filled with ice, I was two, they say, though my age
varies with the telling, sometimes I was a baby,
burning with Scarlet Fever, or pneumonia, or my
toddler's leg suddenly couldn't move, my body
learned to thrive on the fear of illness. Am I ready?
Are you kidding? I've been warming my mask
since childhood.

the trapper & the furrier
by Patricia Carragon

(inspired by Regina Spektor)

2020   a strange   strange year
       like a time bomb   waiting   for breaking news to strike

beasts in filthy cages
       pellets and food   pets from puppy mills

children sleep in soiled cages
       family separation   asylum still out of reach

dystopian predictions   dystopian facts

big business declares war on its workers
       unions   wages   healthcare   live at triage

newspeak from the white house
       twists failure into praise   fiction into history

our self-proclaimed leader plays mobster roulette
       the press   elections   & laws face execution
       he gives carte blanche to an alien dressed as the flu

& the sick keep getting sicker
       with too many fevers   chills   coughs   & losses of smell & taste

death toll rising   ghost towns replace cities
       bodies overflow morgues   the homeless live underground

tests & cures not fast enough
       business as usual for corporate generals

2020   a strange   strange year
       people shut indoors   waiting   not knowing what to believe
       their time bombs   not knowing when to explode

CORONAVIRUS 1, HUMANS 0
by Paula Rudnick

We're all hypochondriacs now,
swallowing our spit to check for throat lumps,
breathing deep and counting up to 10
to make sure lungs still work,
test debunked before we can exhale.

Quacks have set up shop on WebMD
for those who want more info,
pitching vitamins that boost response
to Covid-19 RNA,
claim debunked before we can SKIP AD.

We're underground as mob gone to the mattresses,
Suspecting everyone of packing mucus
Weaponized to take us out
in one damp hocked-up shot
before we have a chance to turn away.

No school, all schools, all day—everywhere,
snowstorm at the door dispensing chill.
No athletes to break sweat for our amusement.
No concerts, theater, dances, no parades
And God forbid—no cruises.

My spouse and I are kids on a first date again.
We hold each other's well-washed, well-dried hands
but we don't kiss. We've social-distanced—
scared of spreading virus through saliva,
spittle only reason we don't scream.

We're watching black and white old classic movies,
Rereading *War and Peace* and *Vanity Fair*.
I've dusted off the Scrabble set and
frozen chicken soup in Ziplock boxes.
Passover, I'll put lamb's blood on the door.

Congested
by Ranney Campbell

we must stay apart
at work in the warehouse
now, under threat of termination

any stray laughter
too loud will draw eyes
of members of the Safety Committee

the rattling metal
rollers sound the same, laden
heavy with orders for those at home;
so heavy that we now work fifty hours; mandatory

and at home, renting
from academics, I am never
alone. they gather here, allowed
loud laughter, because their paychecks never
stopped, so they come to visit every day and watch
the television turned up to best absorb the clashing metal
swords of sci-fi fantasy outside my door; they cannot go in to work
because UCR is shut down to stop the spread, so,so many
others of those, so well employed, are carefree and
laughing on the trails behind my house
where I used to be able

to go
to find
my quiet

The Need is Greed is Want is More
     by Peter Marti

Yesterday, to celebrate 21 days of quarantine
I drove 25 minutes down the Mountain
              for a drive-thru hamburger with fries and a coke
It was delicious
     —even tho the teenager who took my cash and handed me my food wasn't
wearing gloves or a mask

     I wolfed my lunch wondering when we'll ever have
drive-thru COVID-19 testing kiosks this easy
                    or baseball this year…

     I wanted that meal, that rush of pleasant experiences triggering endorphins
in my brain, wanted the murmur of
play-by-play voices on the radio as I ate

I needed it more than I needed isolation and my own cooking
I needed it more than safety—
gambled on my health, the health of those who rely on my health
       —I wanted that taste now
                 more than any future.

The news is shocked our President continues to lie
to punish political foes by denying "Democrat" States
Federal Government stockpiled supplies—privatizing distribution of essential
medical equipment—ensuring those companies who profit, who gouge taxpayers
       ($7 for a .70 cent cotton face mask!)
will contribute to his re-election campaign
     in spite of the blood of thousands washing around his feet
—many of them doctors and nurses treating the infected—
who die because he lied to keep us working, consuming
pretending the Emperor had new clothes for months
instead of preparing for Pandemic

The virus has needs, whispers an "all-clear" the body-need hears

Already today, I crave another trip to town, another type of food I've been missing…
tell myself it's easy to slip away a few hours

   —to give greed what it wants—
to place myself and others in danger for no logical reason
   because habit isn't logical
Insatiable greed isn't logical
   the logic of my amply stocked fridge didn't stop me
   —I could've easily made my own hamburger—
this "wartime" president could have easily commanded the Army and America's infrastructure to respond months ago to save lives

   but greed feeds and eats of its hosts unto Death
    and still that hunger endures.

OP EN   A   LL N IGH T
by Norman Savage

Trying to find sleep
has kept me awake—funny
how these things work...
or don't.
I even tried to stop looking
thinking I'd outfox him; not
a chance.
I watched night after night
the furiously blinking
of colored neon
go off kilter & dance
the dance of St. Vitus.
And other times
I watched myself
and felt gut-punched
like seeing a Hopper painting.

I've believed misery & tragedy
will find you
no matter what you do.
Still, I've barricadded myself
in here for the past month
while that lustful virus
feasted on other hosts
less susceptible than I am.
I've got all the chronic conditions
that the little bugger could hope for.
Once inside, it would make short work of me.

You can learn
about yourself
at any age.
Recently, I'd boast
to all my doctors
& my few friends,
that I'd had a good life:
many scenes, many lovers,

many poems, high highs
& low lows—enough
to expect in this go round.
I was ready.
But now I feel the wisdom
of Auden in his, Musee Des Beaux Arts.
Old men cling passionately to life,
while unexpectedly the young go…
because I don't want to go
anywhere. I have more to read
& more to write. I want
another hot fudge sundae
and the smile of a woman
who sees something
I didn't think was showing.

And so I will watch
the little crack
underneath my door
or my windows
for any sign
of invasion.
I will not go easily;
I'll try to hide
behind the door
sneak up on it,
and knock the motherfucker out.

***

A JUNKY EXPLAINING HIS MOTIVATION AND RATIONALE IN THE MIDST OF A PANDEMIC WITH ALL THE INTELLIGENCE HE CAN BRING TO BARE

Fuck the virus.
I gotta cop.

A Doctor Watching Sunset with His 87-year-old Patient in Wuhan
by Wang Ping

I don't know his name. My friend told me he's from Shanghai, volunteered to go to Wuhan in a lockdown.

I don't how long he's been at his shift, but I feel his hunger and thirst (once you put on the gear, you're locked in 4-6 hours, no food, no water, no bathroom).

I don't know his age, but I know he misses his wife (if he's married), worries about their child's homework, parents' health, their daily meals, their safety…

I can't see his eyes, but I know he's exhausted, mourning his colleagues who fell from the virus and overwork.

Yet when his patient whispers, "I haven't seen the sun for a whole month," he stops the gurney (he's wheeling him to the CT building), says, "I haven't been outside for a month, either. Let's watch."

So the doctor and patient, two strangers, stand still in the empty street, watching the sun setting on Wuhan. 87 years old and sick with the virus, this might be his last glimpse of the sun.

The photo doesn't show their faces, but I see their ecstasy reaching the sky as they bathe in the light, as the hands raise to hope…

The photo doesn't carry their voice, but I hear the symphony of their hearts together: batum, batum, batum…love this life, no matter how old and fragile…love this sunset, even if it were the last…love this earth, our only home…until we know who we are and why we are here…two strangers yet as loving as family can be…as kind as humanity can be…as close to god as the earthlings can reach…at this sunset of Wuhan…through this purity of love….this is what keeps the world going…love…is what will shake 震 us out of our confinement 困…all the lies greed and violence will end in the trashcan of history…but this love will shine as the crown jewel of tomorrow...

Notes:
- The 87 year old musician is recovered from Covid-19 and has returned home.

- The oldest patient Wuhan doctors saved is 102 years old.
- 困：I-ching 51: confinement
- 震: I-ching 47: shake, shock out of the confinement. This is the divination I got on 3-20-2020, "confinement" 51 will be transformed into "shake" through resilience, unity and love.

Watching Sunset Wuhan
by Wang Ping

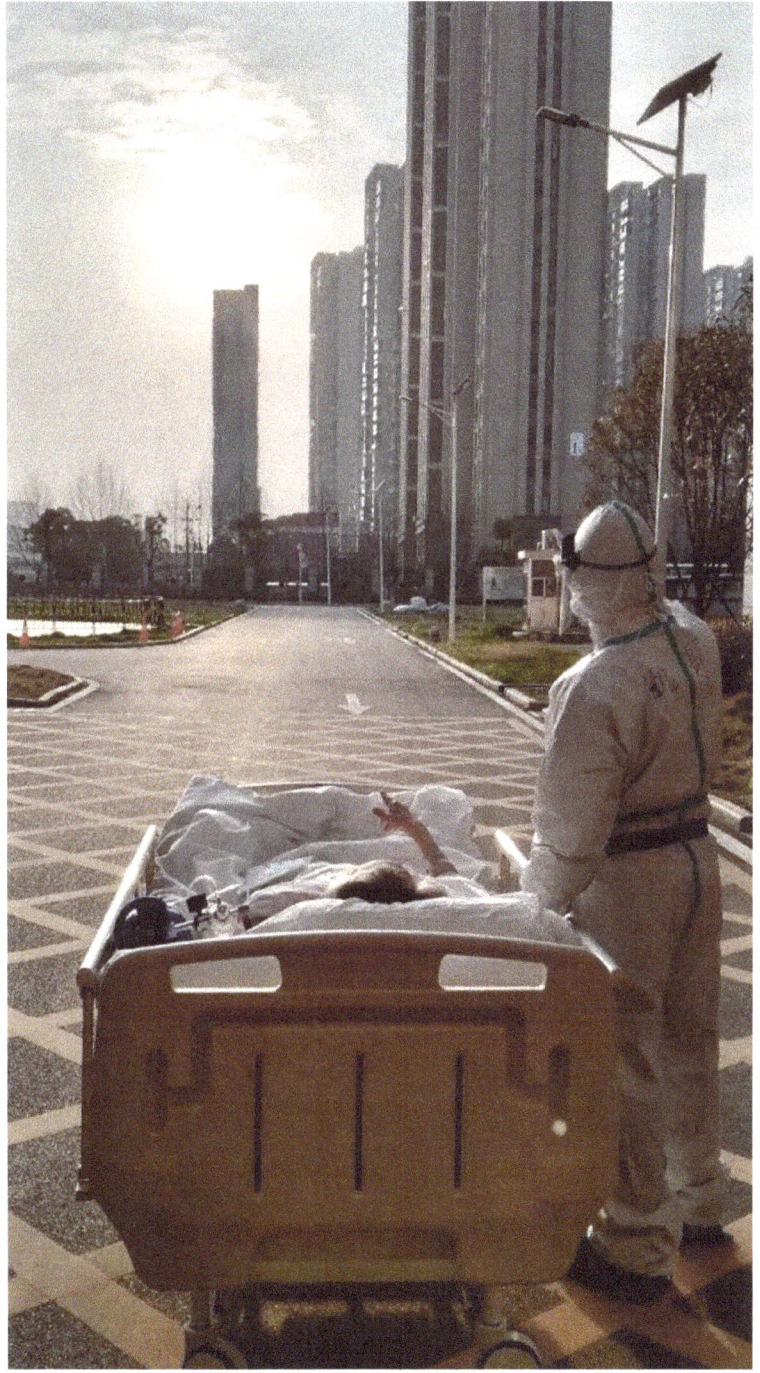

A Litter of Supplies
by Kurt Wit

Today was a hot day.
Sweat dripping,
dropping on lips,
 salt sipping.

Stalled living
 from sitting in lockdown.
 We're all getting sick
 of this timid ground
of not dipping out
 and seeing what life's about.
  Who's out kickin' it?
 Is it inside out?

I left the house today.
Gloves and masks
 littered the way
 to the liquor store
 to see more dismay.

Hot day in LA,
 and people
 are over the covid crisis.
Lined up for ice cream,
 they seem to defy this
whole idea of government advise.
The streets are full again.
  We've rolled the dice.

Don't give me a check
  and expect I'll be inside.
I guess wait for the next
too keep the west confined.

Heat kills the virus,
 and today was hot.
It seems everyone
 had to hit their favorite spot.

BLESS YOU BROTHER
    by Marc Olmsted

Don't believe in a Creator God just because Trump has COVID
it's still a bad dream even if I'm laughing in my sleep
Golden tower still not in ruins
Teens still maskless on city streets
What planet will we resemble in 500 years?
fossil fuel burned on the way to the gun store
how long alt right neighbro thinks COVID a hoax?
black bird solo in the ash-hazed sky
flash fires I have known & loved
Hurricane Kali won't you spare me tonight?
I never did get that Kerouac tattoo
now on the run from the robo-cops
I have confidence in luminous mind
but it's hard to remember Buddha in Hell
man the light bulbs!
Tibetan texts memorized
new poetry sung into space
and instantly forgotten
(somebody else write it down)
"I don't want to be buried/in a pet sematary"
Ramones tune chanted at the camp fire
once upon a time

10/2/20

Trumpenvolk
by Richard Modiano

They eat dead food with
false teeth—
Their buildings have
false fronts—
Their radio and television stations
broadcast dead air—
They kill time as spectators of
false images—
Their corporations trade in false advertising
Their employment "opportunities"
offer only murderous mistreatment
lethal boredom and fatal submission—
They demand that you meet deadlines
They ask you to give up your life for
their countries, their religions, their economies—
They inhabit dead cities and
make false moves going nowhere at all
treading day after day
the same paths of despair—
Their system is organized
by artificial intelligence
and provides only virtual reality—
Their culture will pin you down
and bore you to death
their lifestyle is lifeless—
Their existence is a permanent deadlock
Everything about them is dead and false—
Does the dead end justify the means?
Even their air is conditioned

Different Kind of Dinner
by Tammy Melody Gomez

We try to figure out what to eat
When we're mourning the dead
We concoct recipes for revolution
But forget that we're out of salt
Because we're tear-deprived and
Sweated out through our pores
From July Texas stomp chanting
And marching the path to some
Kind of tasty liberation
That I am trying to cook in my
Poverty line kitchen too. I make some kind
Of dinner using what I have on hand,
Some crunchy cabbage, some cardamom,
The rage within, the salty words,
Add cracked black pepper, leftover onion
I chopped to pieces last night when
The radio news needed another reason
To make me cry. Such a good dish.
After the mural party, and fistbumping
The man who called 911 and got the
Police to do deadly deeds he'll always
Regret, well, there has to be a soup
To purify, maybe sanctify, my ugly cry
As I crack the hard shell of a boiled egg,
It matches my resilience, see how it
Relents, when we need to soften to
Allow a new and decent reset, to sit down
To a different kind of dinner someday.

Day 9 of Self-Isolation
by Kim Dower

I squat on a turquoise blue towel
on the bathroom floor. I remember learning
women in faraway lands and other cultures
give birth this way, but in fact, even here
in America it's a good position for safe birth.
There is no baby inside me but I imagine
an eight pounder plowing through my canal,
my hands poised ready to receive him.
I don't know why I'm doing this except
during this period of Social-Distancing
I think having an infant to care for might be
a fun distraction. When he comes out
he'll be perfect, not even any blood to wash,
no cord to cut, and since I only have cuticle
scissors, that will be a huge relief. He may
even have a full head of hair, slide out holding
his own packet of diapers and perhaps a little bunny
he played with in my womb. It's getting hot in here,
I should crack the window. I don't know how long
it'll take to deliver since there really is no him.
These days are long, and I'm getting bored.
Experts say we should try doing something new.
Baking, for example, or meditating. For now
I will stay put on my turquoise towel,
on the bathroom floor for as long as it takes,
as I wait for my imaginary water to break.

Thoughts After Sitting in Daniel Crocker's Basement
by John Dorsey

i have never been a first responder
a canary in a coal mine

i have always sung too loudly
in times that demanded silence

made off-color jokes
to shield a cough
from being anything more serious

but now i worry about my father
at war with age
& his own failing ears

his heart once lived
in a wiser country

now it only beats
when it feels like it

i worry about everything
my mother puts in god's hands

suddenly it all feels like
one too many bags of groceries
to take into the house.

the ambulances are screaming down 7th avenue again
by George Wallace

maybe we can renegotiate
maybe we can reset the clock
maybe we can climb out the window
(i'll be waiting for you in the bushes,
whistling in the cool night air)
never mind, turn up the news
it's the plague again 24/7
every war's the same, the world
goes radioactive, there's a 650 car
pile up on the snowy interstate (the
numbers doubled overnight)
fire & rescue everywhere,
out come the brave volunteers
from their warm beds (check
the pulse on that one, bill, i'll
clear this lady here's trachea—
afterwards we can share a cigarette)

(i mean war is comradeship, death and survival practically the same)

i was in the car too, you know, just like I was in the war (no not THAT war) I was in the fifth battle of Ypres, 1918, I know the smell of urine in the trenches, and what it means to press your ear to a doughboy's heaving chest—death's happy little rattle—and how flimsy those uniforms they gave us really were, tearaway buttons, and how flimsy the lies, lies! in those days the bastards would tell you anything to hold onto their power, not like now

(and what of the missing stockpiles. and what of the war profiteers, details at 8)

but o the comradeship
o god and country
(i never gave a single
goddamn about no kaiser
or the vietcong)

but o her last kiss on my forehead, cold as the cold clay, the day they sent us off to war (the spanish flu got your grandmother, son, that was in 1919)

and o the cool precision of aerial
bombardment (i was in the last war
too i was a bombardier with a leather
jacket and a lucky red scarf, i lit up
a cool cigarette before the big strike)

it's all fun & games, corporal—hell is for bad guys, not us

war is crushed bone & nicotine

ashes, ashes
we all fall down
(no don't give
the plot
away)

I finally found a chicken
by Kim Dower

after going to four supermarkets:
a decent roaster—we'll get at least
three meals out of it, and if we're quarantined
we can squeeze out a few tacos, even eat
the skin for breakfast. World-coming-to-an-end
lines at the stores, everyone wearing chunky
sweaters, looking up at the sky. People
at the health food store wrapped around the block,
bags of organic cilantro, bottles of Vitamin B-12,
herbal teas shoved into grocery carts. I flee
to my car radio, listen to the press conference,
how many more breathing machines will be
available so doctors won't have to choose
who lives or dies. I smoked all through my teens
and twenties, am intimate with the rich sound
of wheezing deep in my chest, the rattle
of birds dying inside me. At noon every day
wild parrots appear for lunch. I hear them fighting off
the hawks for berries on the trees that shade my house.
I see the parrots fairy-tale green feathers spiking
into the air. Bird blood on my porch.
When my mother got old she couldn't breath.
She had an oxygen tank attached to her as she walked—
hung her purse on it, though her purse had nothing
but a picture of me and my brother and a clump
of tissues. I'm self isolating. Wash my hands
for 20 seconds while singing Happy Birthday.
The man in front of meat Gelson's has 40 rolls
of toilet paper in his cart. I wish the wild parrots
and hawks would practice social distancing.
Less blood on my porch. I don't want my chest
to crackle. I don't want my friends to wheeze
or have high fevers. I'm excited I scored the only
remaining jar of dry roasted peanuts; I'm relieved
my son is older and I don't have to worry his school
is closing. Have inside and outside clothes.
We'll see how this goes. Sleep if you can.

The Coming Darkness
by Luis Cuauhtémoc Berriozabal

After Eavan Boland

I find comfort
in the coming darkness.
It is so dark not
a single moth seeks to
come inside.
The stars are so bright.
This is the moment
I know I made it
through another day.
There is a woman
in my dreams
and there is child,
the child is me.
I shut all the windows.
The pepper tree
is completely black.
I do not go outside.
I shelter in place
like the stars in the sky.
I am no moth
seeking the bright lights.
I remain out of sight.
Things are not like
they used to be.
At dusk
I pray the world
and my surrounding
neighborhood
are much safer
than the day before
as I count
the number
of deaths and
infections
from news reports.

Untitled
by Bryan Scheideck

Off the dead
    by Tammy Melody Gomez

A bloated cat
a stiffened armadillo
a flattened squirrel
that needs to be scraped up
as I bicycle along the insecure streets
today, last week, a month ago,
I'm not sure when.
I try to get my mind off the dead
or dying
and only find it again
and once more
on my restless ride
in this city of groaning spring.
I circle back, could that wiry piece
be a tail, and the bones withered on
the blacktop be formerly white?
Let's call it a baby possum,
just to get the notes wrapped up
for the day, and oh.
A stiff baby bird on the sidewalk
just outside the marketing firm.
No funeral for her either.

At a Time Like This
by Julene Tripp Weaver

new options explode, we download
Zoom, everything moves online,
We review the rules and protocols.

Swamped as usual, my building
being resided by construction
workers, who are essential.

I write a poem a day for National
Poetry Month, feel a surge of
possibility for change, worry

about the election, hold concern for the
homeless, how will they survive—
water tuned off in city fountains,

no public bathrooms open,
parks closed, except they are full—
we are a mess, but life continues

food in my fridge. I add herbs
to strengthen my host immune system,
so when I get this virus I will survive.

My herbal mentor says we will get Covid-19,
reminds us to build our body strong.
Grateful for this life, we must fight back

the way the community gathered
during AIDS. We must learn from them
in this new age. We need ways to win,

like they did in the 80s and 90s.
We cannot lose our advances.
My heart hurts for those who live alone.

The Virus*
by Jennifer Bradpiece

is not a living thing.
The virus can live on metallic
surfaces for nine days.
The virus must be conquered.
The virus must be understood.
The virus is a fraud, a scourge, a wake-up call.
The virus is pulling us together.
The virus may have side effects
like hoax videos of dolphins
jumping canals in Venice.
The virus is tearing us apart.
The virus may induce spontaneous singing
across partially shuddered windows.
The virus is completely under control.
The virus demands stocking
inordinate amounts of toilet paper.
The virus lives on cardboard
for up to two days.
The virus is a call to war.
The virus is like a common flu.
The virus is entirely unprecedented.
The virus is impressively cured
by malaria drugs or Z-Pack.
The virus only affects the vulnerable.
The virus is your neighbor.
The virus is a formidable enemy.
The virus is sponsored by Walmart and Quest.
The virus empties grocery store aisles.
The virus only kills the elderly.
The virus subtracts hospital beds
at great speed.
The virus is indiscriminate.
The virus avoids elementary schools.
The virus attaches to clothing, lungs, and shoes.
The virus comes from bats.
The virus knows where you live.
The virus immunizes Spring Breakers

from social responsibility.
The virus can't be passed by animals.
This virus runs rampant across
continents, overcoats, and imagination.
The virus lives deep within our cell walls.

*a lightly manipulated found poem

Nothing is happening
by Genevieve Legacy

my dog speaks in toenail clicks,
shifts her weight behind the door,
another patient click—
there's no such thing as alone,

Himalayan blackberries
invasive stretching,
reach for more ground,
the meanest thorns
in the neighborhood,

moth white butterfly
crazy wobble flight,
gray fence, black rock wall,
a mailbox squatting across the road,
sticking out its red plastic tongue,

the holly bush has found a new location,
strident prickle-leaves in silhouette,
imagine the sting,

overgrown cascade of ivy,
a black tank-top woman walker,
a Subaru, a dark escalade,
wild grass shoots where my kid didn't mow,
it will take my ferocious choppers
to cut it back,

light shifts from gray to less,
blackberry branch bobs green berries
too soon to pluck, an SUV passes
my window on the street side world,
voyeur of the supra mundane,

dry red shrubs across the street,
ginger bush from 1972
my mother's armpits
a statement of freedom, rebellion?

my own search for what's right—
hairy legs& pits, a prolific bush,
earthy sandal shoes—
no one can tell me what to do.

there's no escape from this house habitat,
20 thousand leagues under the sea,
a Japanese apartment capsule in space,
nowhere to go but the bathroom,
out the window mind wanderer,
black crow line of flight,
straight out of view—

another metallic rolling box,
a dog walking a woman
cell phone pressed to her ear,
my dog's back at the door wondering
where the hell everyone is?

COVID POEM #2
by Suzi Kaplan-Olmsted

There's no such thing as an excess death
Though I'm inclined to admit there are some excess lives
Certainly lives of excess
While some suffer from need
If you have a dead plant
And tie a ribbon on it
You don't have a live plant
You have a dead plant
With a ribbon on it

INMATES
by Celia Bland

The dog floats on the
dark coverlet,
legs straight as
two sides of a handlebar
moustache. She snores.
She curls inwards.
She folds like one of the cardboard boxes
stocked in our basement.
She is kidney shaped now,
a black paisley, a kidney bean.
She is the island
of Bermuda. And we,
two prison hulks, anchor
in her backwater.
You hold my hand
over your heart with both
hands. Leg to leg we float,
pledging health, pledging breath
harboring here off
shore, watched for
but still unseen.

Poetry on the edge of the apocalypse
by Victor Infante

It's just a small "a" apocalypse on the other side of locked doors. The sun is shining on the unkempt lawn, birds are chirping outside my window. There are no hints of shambling zombies in the distance at all. And yet, there's a sharp, indelible pain in the air: small, sudden pinpricks at the base of our necks that come without warning. The antithesis of birdsong.

This is how the world ends/this is how the world ends … you have to look slantwise at everything to understand that it is dying. "Just the facts" are a fraction of the story, and make no mistake, the small "a" apocalypse is the only story to tell right now. It infects more than blood: It has infected our economics and politics, although those things had preexisting conditions. It bleeds through our television and music, upends our cinema, decimates our theater. It sits down to dinner with our families, hovers over children at school in the living room, haunts the floors of nursing homes.

Plain language is insufficient for the enormity of this moment, where the newscasts feel like dire weather reports from foreign countries, spoken in a language almost recognized. You catch every third word or so: *Emergency,* they say, then later *stimulus,* then *tantrum.* The listener fills in the empty spaces with the word *fear,* until they either realize that it's *all* empty spaces, or the fear itself becomes too overwhelming to bear.

Still, amid the tempest of numbers and the newsprint bonfire, there is an unassailable truth that we see at the grocery store, where the masked cashier you've known for a decade smiles with her eyes and takes a half-step backward as you approach the register. You understand the language of the unconscious recoil, as you understand the bellyache absence when you see friends and coworkers on video screens, remember their distinct presence in a room, how even indifference used to have as texture. Now we think of them as television: eagerly awaited, the way one awaits any narcotic that numbs pain.

Poetry is the only form of speech we have that meets this need to acknowledge that we are more than unemployment statistics and death tolls. If this is the end of the world, our stories need to be more than whimpers in the darkness. As our nations and businesses are revealed as pantomime, that ache and light that stirs in our chest, that thing we see shining in each other, is the only thing that's definitely real.

A middling tide
by Kate Robinson

Sudsy stagnant seaweed floating touching bottom
Dinghies moored with seaweed-clung ropes
Neon green tethers in water reflecting grey clouds

I'll, I'll follow you…

My favorite café is full
You can't sit inside anymore so everyone crowds the outdoor tables
But there aren't enough in tourist season

A blue cloth mask tumbleweeds down the quay
A man sneezes into his elbow
The old woman on the bench next to me yells her response into a cellphone
Loud pants to match

Wet cough behind me
110 new cases in 5 days in Finistère
Maybe 300 total during confinement?

Seagulls milling above
A family of four goes
back up the boat launch
looking at their feet
Loose gait of people with nowhere to be
The ice cream delivery man
Is the only person walking with purpose
pushing his yellow cart

Untitled
by Bryan Scheideck

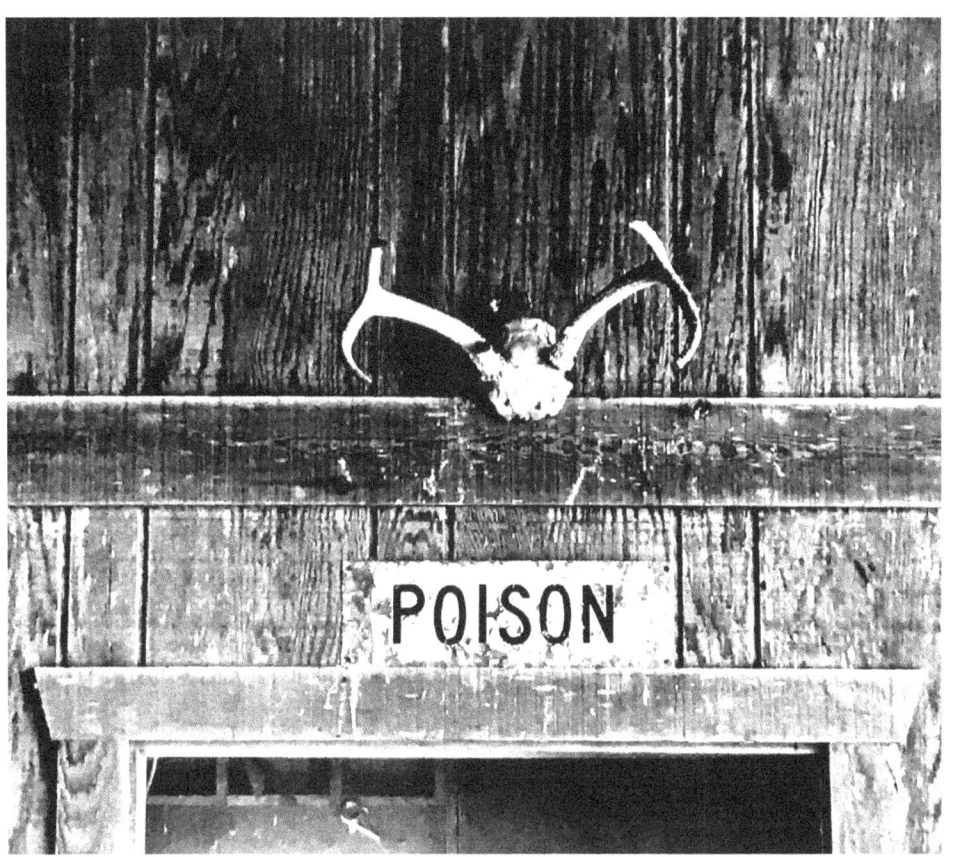

Lessons Learned During a Pandemic
by Connie Owens Patton

Reality stars can't run countries

Eyes tell stories when
Masked mouths trap conversation

It's possible to live separately together

Square footage shrinks
When leaving isn't voluntary

Television causes anesthesia
Music is the cure

The sun is therapy

Nothing replaces
The warmth of my mother's hands

Names are not necessary
To mourn the dead

spring happened without men in it
by George Wallace

Absent of commuter trains and contrails against the blue,
the wing-tail festival began, two glorious weeks of spring
without men in it, lord love the acorn juggler and the
high wire act, furry aerial divers in every oak, everyone
(save old raccoon in his winter coat, overturner of garbage
pails) grateful as a creature of God can be, celebrating
the news (and all along the cornfields and musty in the
barn, mice made nest of seat cushion and engine block);

The cold brown stalks of yesteryear stood unshorn,
mannequin-bare the feral housecat made his jungle
moves (stalking the elusive North American rabbit)
and blue jays held new commerce with the crows,
it was the red dawn of robins again, a rosy peace
broke out among the animals, blue wind hollared
through violets and purple crocuses, there was frogs

In every pond, sunlight quarreled with shade, croakers
croaked, wrens nested in any damn eave they pleased,
and a pair of wild ducks waddled down Main Street USA
unmolested, it was like Windmill Lane all over again;
nature undeterred; it was the restoration of the old
order, everyone (including hawk on the wing and fox
in his lair) stopping to reexamine their plans

Against the return of man

crema-oratory
by Marc Olmsted

"Sorry
we're cursed"
misread sign in storefront

Barbecue flames in the night
the cro mag drummer
pretends in his front yard
with plump girlfriend
(& her son who looks like a serial killer
or he shot John Lennon)
that the world is not on fire

* virus eve *
hang your latex booties
on the crematory chimney

"isolation nation"
catchy MSNBC news
the closed captions
misspell, sound off
"we're in violation"

4/15-16/2020

Eudaimonia
by Viggo Mortensen

Before
dread
before
being
invited
she
wins
trick's
staying
thriving
feeling
something
helping
someone
something
bloom
imagining
that
while
she
rebuilds
collapses
each
uneasy
breath
passing
storm
sunup
seedling
flowering
magnolia
wisp
drought
eruption
extinction
decaying
drowning

twisted
thorny
burning
bramble
cracked
ochre
clay
sheltered
shorn
dormant
devours
devoured
trails
putrid
rainbows
airborne
assassins
takes
you
in
murderous
embrace
blurs
seasons
trembling
budding
stinking
sinking
settling
stone
cold
sand

All going to die
All going to die

Loveliest
spring
recalled

rain
sun
rain
sun
paired
day
night
lambent
daybreak
glorious
radiance
ennobles
soaking
ditches
magpie
mondays
whippoorwill
wednesdays
exalting
succession
parting
songs
insistent
pullulating
reconfigured
native
terrain
innocuous
billowing
mist
deep
verdant
riverine
absolution
nooning
drifting
unified
fused
inseparable

passerine
days
follow
iris
evenings
eudaimonia
attained
malice
implausible
just
then

All going to die
All going to die

Some
learn
what
rots
when
around
edges
thrives
why
who
leaves
first
how
insides
work
what
we
are
she
was
why
we
go
she

stays
some
bravely
while
away
days
sifting
dust
knowing
these
flickerings
cannot
match
her
incendiary
reach
understanding
our
puny
vexing
thankless
perishable
aberrations
offer
mere
second
rate
parasites
always
late
to
the
bone

All going to die
All going to die

Who
thought

this
world
anything
but
hers
why
conceive
envision
promote
victory
through
guile
science
faith
will
magic
no
age
of
reason
avails
no
predication
signified
no
wild
guess
aimless
divination
sways
steers
her

La Escencial
by Marisela Norte

Doing Nothing
by Luis Cuauhtémoc Berriozábal

I used to find
doing nothing
the thing to do
when I had things
to do, places
to go to, like
work, the park, or
the record store.
Now that I have
to do nothing
but stay home, I
find it hard to
just do nothing.
I read. I clean
a little. I
eat too much. I
watch tv a
little bit more.
I watch the news
to get an idea
of how this world
is shaping up.
It will not get
better any
day soon if the
human beings
continue to
listen to lies
and keep going
out infecting
everybody.
Doing nothing,
staying in place,
is what we all
need to learn to
do to survive.

Just touched
    by Tammy Melody Gomez

Wow, look at us [in this foto] in such close proximity.
These days, when I watch online movies I have this instinct of care & concern when I see the characters walking too close together.
Giving each other kisses on the cheek.
Touching or picking up things that someone else just touched.
I'm noticing what I notice, and am trying to track these mental-emotional changes in my thoughts and perceptions.

And it is not lost on me that I have decided to re-watch and study the works of Japanese director Yasujirō Ozu. His characters, especially in his early films, DEFINITELY do well with social distancing.
And sadly, too well with the emotional distancing too.

tldr: Please NOTICE what YOU NOTICE. Especially now.

Self-Isolating Dog
by Kim Dower

My son tells me Gwen is bored
so he forces her to watch squirrel
videos. She's obsessed,he tells me,
growls and barks as she watches
them run up and down trees, sends me
pictures of her glued to the action,
close-ups of her almond shaped eyes,
shining, staring, her funny ears twitching.
She barely moves, just watches, waits.
I'm not bored,just anxious. When I see
a squirrel on the sidewalk coming a little
too close, I cross the street fast, cover my
mouth, stop breathing. I'm obsessed by
cleaning the counter with alcohol, the mole
that's appeared on the back of my calf,
obsessed with the masked man across the way
who looks into my window. Will I awaken
with that little dry cough? I long to be a dog
like Gwen, be her friend, sit beside her
on the couch, watch virtual squirrels jump
from branch to branch, fight her for treats,
nap on my very own fear-free doggie bed,
nothing surrounding me but love;
nothing to kill but time.

Siren Song for Jacksonville
by Eileen Carole

This is not the last summer day.
The ebb and tide may call you
But it's only the siren's song.
Do you really want your future dashed upon the rocks?
Blue water has its lure.
The call of the surf can sweep you up.
The sun may shine your name.
But if you're not in this day
The sun will come again.
The sailors of Greek mythology felt it impossible to ignore;
Called to distraction by the song.
Be stronger. Don't listen.
Heed the advice of the powers that be.
Stay home.
The beach will be there next month.
It will even be there next year.
And the sun will shine again
And you can water frolic the day away
Or you can submit to the siren's song
And submerge into the Covid depths.

Being, Human
by Heather Pease

Soon we will count
the dead by who we
know or knew.
Soon it won't matter if
your backyard is full
of leaves.
Life will be recorded as
after…

and I don't know which
statistic I will be
part of, or how to prepare for
anything—except breathing.

Monsters in closets don't seem
as scary. At least they
are home, and safe.
Each night a survival, but
the clock ticks on. I've stopped
setting the alarm.

Is anyone ever really
prepared—when the end
could be tomorrow? These thoughts
are now rational.
So is admitting
fear, as we shelter in place;
reminiscing about hugs
we may never
share again.

There are people we
will want to reach
out to—but don't.
Even in a pandemic
things will remain
unresolved.

Regret will be a list too
long. Nothing will ever
be the same. Soon
we will stop
being in denial
of what is our own
fault. Wait
who am I kidding? We're
human.

Take Your Medicine this Time so You'll Know What to Do Next Time!
    by Aqueila M. Lewis-Ross

There's no time to panic!
This isn't that fake news you heard so much about!

The baby still needs to be fed.
She's watching how you move
And groove within the times we are in.
Her smile is proof.
You can rest assured that everything will be alright.

Cuz you've been here before remember?
That fire you ran away from as it cleansed the earth.
Displacing.
Rebuilding.
And replacing plans.
You can't see it now, but your blessing will come.
But for now it's the time for testing.
A race to prove who is really fit.
Not all can make it across the finish line.
Somehow folks have forgotten.
There's no negotiating your fate.
When your number is called you will answer.
It's the time for resting if you can.

The homeless and unhoused are your teachers, ask them.
The babies are your leaders, follow them.
Cuz they know the answers.
And mama earth has the medicine to heal.
Broken Bodies.
Broken Hearts.
Broken Minds.
Broken Friends.
Broken Loves.

Some will finally pick up that Big Book searching for what it says.
Remember when you put it away.
On time out.

Or for safe keeping.
There it was buried in piles of boxes.
You promised you'll come back to it someday.
Well, the time is finally here!
When the waters flood sickness rushes in.
Demanding needed change.
Disasters teach lessons.
Helping you remember what made you fall in love.
And what friendships and kindness really looks like.

Take your medicine!
Rest and get ready!
Because after this,
if there's a next time,
you'll know exactly what to do.

Touchless Sonnet
by Lynne Bronstein

"I need a hug." It's what we've always said.
We still need hugs but now is not the time.
It's stop, not go; the light has changed to red.
The walls are up and there's no place to climb.
We're going nowhere. Safe within a room,
We type our love or speak it on the phone.
Friends and lovers meet and greet on Zoom,
But many have to face the day alone.
Look left, look right, don't walk across the lines.
Breathe in, breathe out. Be careful with your breath.
Live for the moment and for future times
And make good use of all the time that's left.
I hope that I can spend my hours in grace
And bring good vibes to all that I embrace.

Hibernate.
by Laura Thurlow

Post-hibernate
Post buzz words post
Proposed normals new
Post do I, don't I stifle breath
With fabric I bought to make a dress
But instead have used for armour
Post spring-time
When the flowers beckoned me and I ignored them
Post worry, rekindle old flames or light new ones
Become desirable, become infinite
Preach enlightenment when all you mean
Is you've come to forgive yourself
For you had been such good company
All that time
Seek company, and re-learn speech
Oui, je sais, comment ça va ?
I've loved you all this time and not yet known
How wonderful you were while you were far away
Contemplate embrace, and learn it like an infant
Good touch, bad touch, cheek-to-cheek
Let the sun kiss you, let it warm you
Let the ocean take you, let it cleanse you
Admit that you did nothing, learned nothing
Became nothing, you spent all those months nursing yourself
You had taken on so much blame
And now you can't even find her in the mirror
That wretched hateful woman
Post-hibernate, begin to smile at strangers on the street, again
Let your body learn of joy, let the lovely beckon you
And shed the skin you filled with holes
And throw out all your matches
There is not a fire to start there
Is already something burning
Something organic, within you
If you'd listen to your heartbeat
Post-hibernate, if it happens, when it happens
You will be so warmed by it

Post Beltane, missing all the spring rites
When it happens, when it happens
There will have been such a long winter
And you will know how to survive.

Wash Your Hoofs
by Rachel Ikins

65 Bucks
by Luis Cuauhtémoc Berriozabal

Paid the parking
ticket online.
Money wasted
due to no good
parking spots in
Los Angeles.
They would charge you
for the air you
breathe if they could.
It is not like
the air is all
that good for your
health with all the
smog everywhere.
Sixty-three bucks
plus two dollars
charge for paying
online. I saw
I just missed the
the meter cop
by five minutes.
I hope they spend
that money well.
I know I could
have bought like 8
masks and some hand
sanitizer
if it was in
stores. If they did
not want us all
to die or to
get others sick,
they would give us
the things we need
for free. Is it
cheaper to let
us die? Have they

done the math in
Washington? I
know they can count
how much is in
their pocket books.
They do not have
the slightest of
ideas how
far sixty-five bucks
can go for us.

This Is for the Birds!
by Mark States

(for Arroe Collins)

Birds have always been good at social distancing.
See a human walking up the street toward them,
they fly away, or with stutter-steps
make certain to stay a good 6 to 10 feet away
before darting off within some cluttered shrubbery
or underneath a parked, dusty white 2008 Chevy
that probably runs no faster than birds can.
Birds find safe spaces on the down-low
when they choose not to fly to pine tree across the street
or wire strung like a tightrope between metal power poles.

Yet recently, more and more I've noticed
these birds *not* flying away as I approach.
Standing on the lawn they are, with twig or debris
in their beaks, just watching me, looking into my eyes.
I wonder if they have remarked to themselves
there are far fewer humans out here, fewer
metallic beasts roaring down these streets,
if they sense in their souls the way an arthritic knee
aches when barometric pressure changes
before a rainstorm, that something ominous
is going on in their world.

Birds from a safe social distance stare at me,
and when I happily greet them with a "Hello birdie!"
they tilt their heads as dogs do when you say something
to them that does not quite make sense.

I find this interspecies interaction invigorating,
a moment to realize that not everything is
chaos and danger in our world.
Life is more than being cooped up
within a cage of drywall and glass windows
yearning for the freedom of sun and sky.
I walk away from this bird, joking to myself,
I hear the top tune on their billboard perch these days
is "Where Have All the French Fries Gone?"

malachite, gemstone too heavy to bear
by George Wallace

you are socked in, night grips you like an old jet liner in foggy weather, no flights out and the thrum of the empty airport corridor after midnight churns in your ear—New York City the great city you were born in clings to you, and New York City is emptying out, and the people with it, not a soul on fire or ice in this town, the streets in the deep emptiness of fog, from the 24th floor the streets of the city seem even more long and glum, you noticed it from the yellow taxi, you noticed it when you first walked in, your heart slowed to a stop when you first saw him, (turned to the window to stop the dizziness from setting in)—

(how much time has he even got left, doctor,
the old man lying there)

no sign he recognizes you or the flowers you brought, useless, can't even bring them in

in his sullen going he is a stone of transformation, call him malachite, a gemstone too heavy to bear, and you? call yourself a fool for rushing to his side, wearing a heartstone engraved with disbelief and childhood regret, caught in the throat of love's necessary labors, wanting to run down the long corridor (a gurney rolling past, o muffled rubberwheel), turned twice around your neck a gold crucifix—

life is not gold, it is a green petal that unfurls and unfurls until one day it won't unfurl, it is a brownstick used for swatting at ants

(how much longer nurse? the nurse struck dumb),

even the doctor when he finally arrives seems tongue-tied (we cannot be certain, he says, but please don't give up hope)—

(the cool of windowglass against my forehead)

hope! what hope can cure this? hopeful news from Wuhan, where the virus has maybe stopped spreading; hopeful news from Italy, where the people are singing each other lullabies; hopeful news from Washington, if you are willing to believe literally anything you are told (wash your eyes and ears, don't touch

your lips to candlesticks)—
 but little left in room 2414 where hope and death
are clear as the gossamer that seals the old man's
lips and covers the old man's watery eyes, (those
aquamarine eyes of his, still so beautiful);

and his closed eyelids, yellow as forsythia, yellow that
pales to white, and a hint of purple—New York City at
dawn, (the mean old sky refusing to let go of the gray)

The Smarmy Thorn Must Die
by Marc Zegans

There stood a selfish king from the east
A king of lies, small-handed, vulgar, low
And he had broken his solemn oath
To share what he did know.

He took a plough and plough'd truth down
A clod to his power wed
And he had broken his solemn oath
As his countrymen fell dead.

But the Spring, he said, was anon
And the cases soon would fall.
The numbers rose up again
And cruel cast their deadly pall.

The opening of Summer sultry
Declared he, was near at hand
The market would regain its heights
And on played the Foxish band.

The voting Autumn did appear
Fore rasp-breathed dying souls
Their families each sorrow laid
As the smarmy king cajoled.

His colour orange faded grey
He descended into rage
His band of former fellows
Left his thick head upon the stage.

Twisted as he writhed un-tanned
Blame outward sent: "Them,"always, "not I"
As cast they paper ballots, shouting
The smarmy king must die.

The distemper's progress was allayed
And kind folk did again see sky

While children played in the park
Once the smarmy king did die.

Now let us toast what nigh must pass
Each person that does survive
And fall to obscurity, then
The smarmy thorn that died.

Pandemic
by Carolina Rivera Escamilla

My usual thoughts on paper almost never flow in a coordinated way. I let thoughts bounce as though they were a branch with a monkey swinging wide, up, down, sometimes touching ground. Buds of ideas demand that my human hands steady the branch of scattering thoughts. Mind-hands pull the thought-filled branch down for closer examination, maybe pet it, comfort it into slow steady sways, not so much for me but for those who will read me.

COVID-19 settled and got real, at least metaphorically, into this, my mind, when government 'experts' wisely exerted power to announce the wisdom of staying at home, washing hands, wearing a mask, keeping six feet away from people, or otherwise risking death. Already focusing, concentrating on writing was becoming quite difficult. My university and foundation programs disappeared, along with my gratifying fourth wall of grouped audiences. Social desperation zoomed in search of poets, word-filled writers trying to break into spirit groups across oceans, seas, freeways, from landscapes and bodies of water I could only look at on maps. COVID-19 took away physicality, replaced it with two-dimensional virtuality.

My mind transformed into restlessness, like autumn's last fly moving from room to room waiting for cold weather. My thoughts turned into bumble bees with no-blossoms-so-no-honey-to-create, even though I was still trying to ingest invisible waters every second. I tried sanity through breathing exercise. In isolation, thoughts grew like cells in a laboratory dish; would I have to let them die? Like a masochist, I reread cancellations, every lost spring and summer invitation. Francis intervened with a calming "Relax", more effective than my breathing.

I started calling family far and wide. Conversations mixed with unsolicited advice, recalled our long-ago surreal confinements during the civil war, speculated about this job- and future-killing virus, feared the loss of loved ones without proper goodbyes. Conspiracy-theories bloomed, too: "they" send us to hide in fear so "they" can rob last treasures of The Amazons, or control all fresh water. And as we talk and talk through our dystopic misgivings, like this, I tell conspiracy-friends that my son, a freshly minted Biology PhD, assures me that the virus is real. It can make us sick in a breath and kill in a matter of days. It forces us to cancel our Baltimore trip for his May graduation, turned virtual as well.

In late March, I zoomed with writers for the first time. Soon virtual colonies of swarming intellect came buzzing. ZOOM came for me with reading events around the world in Spanish and English. In March, neighbors also joined my husband and me for 8 p.m. gatherings on our street making noise, playing instruments, even doing socially distanced poetry readings. Words came out like this: "Distance makes us feel magical moments, but wondering and wandering virtually feels like losing sunflower petals before springtime has even arrived."

And by April, thoughts still evading paper, I got news: "Mom, I got the Saul Roseman Award for outstanding dissertation!" My son has been my soul's libation. His words balanced my mind. And a gig landed from a museum to write a poem based on a painting. My thoughts took me to watch nature with a renewed consciousness. I listen to the wind kissing a silenced leaf that falls in my head. A poem starts coming out:

In the bedroom, I seclude myself for hours.
A white blanket mummifies my body.
My eyes follow plaster traces on the cream ceiling.
I wish for wings to go see my son, my father, all my family,
                                              fragmented
by civil war, postwar, by gangs taking over El Salvador,
and now this.

Confinement does not faze me.
I've gone through curfews, exile,
                            believe me,
curfews and exile prepare for confinement.
What scares me is the arrogant despot
Protecting money over lives,
(Mis)leading this country like so many others,
Killing people for profits.
Memories come like pulses of light,
fireflies in these days of lockdown.
I see mother gathering her children
to save them from a military hand.
I see father trying to steal a piece of sky
as a roof to hide his children who are emigrating…
running from the bullets.
I remember my brothers hiding in car trunks,
To cross the border from Mexico to the USA.
remember migrants crossing in crowded broiled
spaces of tractor-trailers.

Many died.
Caged children in detention centers pop in,
thoughts buzzing in the air in this anxious sleeping space,
the weight of a leaf falls,
butterflies circulate near wind chimes,
A cloud passes by.
Hummingbirds are stationed on a wire.
I hear the faucet running water
or is it the garden hose?
Francis is washing aging agile hands
for the tenth time in an hour.
His hands flutter under water,
and I wonder whether they will grow waterfalls,
instead of dissolving the worldwide enemy
under his nails.

Confinement comes with other memories:
Bombardment by hysteric social media,
Facebook, CNN, cable channels, newspapers
announcing like coroners of the world,
COVID19 is coming! It's coming!
It's already close!
stay home, wash your hands,
hot water, alcohol, soap…
Pandemic, pandemic, virus, pandemic,
COVID-19 is killing tens of thousands in Europe,
now it's here!
                    In New York City, in Seattle,
                    Los Angeles,
CNN flashes images of bodies
buried in a mass grave,
a communal grave, new angels for our Queen.

I fell sick for long days,
Depressed,
must have the virus.
How many times has the suspicion crossed my mind …

I meet new people in Zoom readings.

I reconnect with some I have not heard from in years.
When protests come, I scream the worst virus is Racism.

    July comes, and I breathe a different consciousness. I step out in the morning light, smell orange blossoms, see tiny hummingbirds sway around Francis' tiny garden. Lizards have lost their fear of cars, slip throughout its middle and edges. On my long walks, I see a human walking at some distance, our faces covered. We evade each other. Later, when we both get home, we will run hot water with soap over our hands.

Cthonic? Could Be a Cough
by Amélie Frank

This year, it is all about breathing in parentheses.
Open parens, left ear loop, half a smile,
close parens, right ear loop, other half of smile,
between loops, sheer moiré spans the width of your face.

Open parens, left ear loop, half a smile.
Who weaves, who measures your days, who casts them off?
Between loops, sheer moiré spans the width of your face,
now barrier, now suspension bridge, now lifespan.

Who weaves, who measures your days, who casts them off?
Who will give you space to breathe the fatal air?
Now barrier, now suspension bridge, now lifespan,
the threads rya-rya-rya'ed by three nimble sisters

who will give you space to breathe the fatal air.
New masks are woven to the R&B tune "Games People Play,"
the threads rya-rya-rya'ed by three nimble sisters—
oscines, weaverbirds, keepers of odd time signatures.

New masks are woven to the R&B tune "Games People Play."
The eldest sister calls it, "19 notes per measure."
(Oscines, weaverbirds, keepers of odd time signatures.)
"Quarter note keeps the beat."

The eldest sister calls it, "19 notes per measure.
1 the alpha, 9 the omega. All set for the next life.
Quarter note keeps the beat."
Ever the middle child, the Alloter curses.

"1 the alpha, 9 the omega?! All set for the next life??!!
Γαμώτο! Το 19 είναι ένας πρώτος αριθμός!"
(Ever the middle child, the Alloter curses.)
The Inflexible snips, stubs the thread to her tongue.

"Γαμώτο. Το 19 είναι ένας πρώτος αριθμός.
Αρκετά. This is God's perfect order."

The Inflexible snips, stubs the thread to her tongue.
"This is the closing of their season."

"Αρκετά. This is God's perfect order."
(The eldest has always nursed a soft spot for dumbass mortals.)
"This is the closing of their season."
Inflexible Baby chews the thread like a cheroot and knots it

The eldest has always nursed a soft spot for dumbass mortals.
Close parens, right ear loop, other half of smile.
Inflexible Baby chews the thread like a cheroot and knots it.
This year, it is all about breathing in parentheses.

Ancient Greek for "Fuck this shit! 19 is a prime number!"

strange blues on my phantom
by Marc Olmsted

strange quiet
strange COVID
strange President
in charge of looting
his people
keep moving
the tear glasses
cloud the
horses
the bible
held by
a demon

Scooters
by Jim McDonald

A few moments in the time of Corona
by Rafael Alvarado

I get a nitro at Starbucks
On my way to court appointed therapy
Hasn't made a dent in my nature
I see a sign
Feeling disillusioned
Talk to Jesus
So I think about it
I'm stupid I want a conversation
I want answers
I don't
Want to get frustrated
Waiting for signs that he heard me

So instead
I suck it up
2 weeks the gyms closed
I'll find a way
Not to lose my mind
2 weeks paid
No work

The world starts crying
I don't have anything big enough
To wipe its tears

A woman at the market has a facemask
Made of glitter
I can't keep my mouth shut
I insult her and her boyfriend
I hate stupid people

I'm an ass
I know it
But I'm a loyal ass

I ask an as on facebook
If shes ok

Cause I tend to carry
My past in suit cases
Leave them closed most days
Other days I check
Love still floats in the wind
It just doesn't land anymore
You cant change the past
You can respect that it was
No rewriting

Embrace yesterday for a moment
Then let it go

blue cat at dawn
by George Wallace

Sandburg had it right (in virus
time) dawn sits like a blue
cat outside the hosp-
ital window with
blue whiskers
(I am blue fog,
I am a white star
in heaven) peering in
(I am a set of car keys that
has disappeared through
a hole in the world)
(a shadow creeps down
the long corridor) I am
an unopened envelope
l am an unanswered
letter, unexpressed
emotion (laid out
on the surgical
table I am a get
well quick card,
read slowly)—
O! see how they
run the masked
young faces (like
mischievous children)
daylight shudders to
life one more time
(O! Lord give us this
day) (so like a sword run
through the gut, a scabbard
& blade, rudely plucked
from the throat of
heaven) Lord
let this day
approach
humbly
on

little blue
cat-feet
(feel the
first shaft
of light)

The Body Snatcher
by Marc Olmsted

Karloff & Lugosi
horror actors on TV
19th Century surgery
cadavers I have known & loved
the little girl can't walk
in her Victorian wheelchair
I am old, in white face
hiding from COVID
my wife sick
but not with the virus
my wheelchair
is the television
watching protest across the nation
ashamed
my wheelchair is shelter-in-place
kneeling on the neck of George Floyd
my wheelchair is sensible
like shoes & a tie
my wheelchair is a noose
my wheelchair is an unraised fist
my wheelchair is a plate glass window
looking at the plague world
my TV is an iron lung
it can't hear me inside
screaming

Untitled
by Eleanor Kedney

I have more time for peacemaking.
Bare feet on kitchen tile, a bent knee
between cat and dog, nose-to-nose
for the first time. Her stare-downs,
hisses, claw curls, his sixty-pound body
pressed into my leg. I'm peacemaking
mostly with myself—the pulled wagon
of papers, the deed to the sold house
where my childhood roves each room,
an x-ray of my mother's spine,
bones thin as mine, my father's wallet
still carries my high school picture.
My brother's baby hair in an envelope.

I wake to birdsong and mild sun, hungry.
By noon I sit in a chair, arms
crossed—new virus cases dot a graph,
a long white semi turned morgue,
along its parked wheels daffodils bloom.
A black beetle zooms up the wall.
They come inside for water,
our desert spring with its early heat.
What's the name of the Ella jazz tune
that makes me want to rock my hips?
Play *that* instead of the news.

A friend walks her old dog
while I walk mine a road-width apart.
I'm not using the word *weary*
when talking about the pandemic.
The letter *p*, a voiceless bilabial stop.
We pass the row of mailboxes,
evening spirals down,
Venus alights in a less-polluted sky.
Lizards' quick bursts as the blacktop cools.
Three new buds on a cholla cactus
that copes and adapts every summer.

The earth itself has grown quieter,
and when I'm silent,
I can hear the singing of the stars above.

Immersive Theater
by Tammy Melody Gomez

I have a mother
She is 4 foot ten
& full of grace
Trunk full of food
About once a month

My fridge is full

I have a sister
Who had sepsis in June
Words on a page
Comfort me

No hospital visit for me
& Simon,
I trust he's truthful
And we'll vent a (little) later

Glad
I have a nephew
More than a rumor
We Zoomed one time
So I have seen him for real
He and I ate pizza on Berry
3 weeks B.C. (Before COVID)

Aqui Estoy Mi Amor
by Marisela Norte

What Gives Hope
by Julene Tripp Weaver

The miracle might be we emerge from this
to a better world with a clearer vision, higher
priorities, closer connections to each other;

that we might learn to live together in peace,
a new emphasis on healing the pain
our ancestors perpetuated with slavery.

We've been isolated in this pandemic, thrown
online to meet. Contact our most important
social soothing, cyber space not the body-

to-body we yearn, nuance obscured with distance.
Awash in protest with condoned police violence,
still, some are hopeful. It is clear now, essential

workers are expendable. We are here to return
our blood to the earth by rule of their volition,
let us be drained like a slaughtered deer. Or,

we'll die in hospitals from Covid-19, intubated.
In the streets we have always died. Our blood,
our breath obstructed with no mercy, a clamp

on the poor with no clout—unlike those who
prosper from crisis. We, the little ones with jobs lost,
income gone, family dead from systemic violence,

these pressured times we've always lived through.
Yet some have hope and fire to burn, the young
who only knew Obama their first eight years.

They follow behind, yet-to-lead on the front line
of change that is coming. And oh, to have
their fresh votes, their wisdom, their vision.

FOR THE WORLD DEAD
by Neeli Cherkovsky

heart and soul, skull and bones
what are you not doing right?
why do you look through stained glass?
you must be mute or loud,
you go to bed in a death shroud
you lost your light in a teeming crowd
I sailed on your thoughts
I ate from the bowl of silence
hard work takes its toll, oh science!
soul and word, letter and bite
what did you do all night in the crowded emergency ward?
I feel you in the prison of night
a tambourine man for your elegy
his tintinnabulations seem to fit
your crown of thorns, why? who?
you were born to suffer this way
it seems, an infinite you pronounced
dead, one memory less, a free bed
even a strong Buddha fails, an old
lady in Rome, a cop in Detroit, the last
master of ambition, residual magic,
will you turn off the lights? oh leave
a candle to burn, the raven will march
down from a promontory for needed
rest, you will die, the furthest star
will send dead sight, a prism might
be your vision lying mute, or gripping
an attendant's aura, do you feel?
bone and heart, nerve and lung,
what brought you here? all power
to the ghost of your hopes, may you
find a desert of peace as you cross over
the ruins and execute a maze,
from Carthaginian stones and
small business loans, from idols
in your head, from sick politics,
 we are only able to salute

the world dead, and pour air
on their heads
alas, poor noble prince and
damsel, old man riddled with bad
health, millions without food
because so many are dead, even
our libraries die, the cathedral roof
goes up in flames, who do you
blame? what matter power
 or fame? for the world blessed in
life and death, we will never see
the end of it
head and hand, song and lance,
exquisite dancer, angry dreamer,
fight for another day and night,
our lives are a gift from a blue
breeze, we live with ants and
bumble bees, we skid, we
rap, we cringe, we are so scientific and
skilled, we flood ourselves in
rapture and let the demos in

by Consuelo Flores

Contributors

Born in 1965, **Rafael FJ Alvarado** has been producing poetry events in Los Angeles's for over 25 years. Widely published, Rafael was an editor/publisher of the legendary zine *sic vice and verse* for over ten years. He hosted the World Wide Word radio network for three years and interviewed dozens of poets from across the globe. Rafael's grandmother wrote poetry and his granduncle was Luis Cardoza y Aragon the renown Guatemalan poet.

*

Elaine Barnard's collection of stories, The Emperor of Nuts: Intersections Across Cultures was published by New Meridian Arts and noted as a unique book on the Snowflakes in a Blizzard website. She has been nominated for the Pushcart Prize, Best Small Fiction and Best of the Net.

*

Born in Mexico, **Luis Cuauhtémoc Berriozábal,** makes his home in Southern California and works in the mental health field in Los Angeles. His most recent poetry book, Make the Water Laugh, was published by Rogue Wolf Press and can be ordered on Amazon.

*

Celia Bland is the author of three collections of poetry and the co-editor of *Jane Cooper: A Radiance of Attention* (U of Michigan). She lives in Kingston, NY.

*

Jennifer Bradpiece was born and resides in the multifaceted muse, Los Angeles. She has interned at Beyond Baroque, and project collaborations with multimedia artists feed her passion. Jennifer's poetry has been widely published and nominated for a Pushcart Prize. She is the author of *Lullabies for End Times* (Moon Tide Press, 2020), and *Ophelia on Acid* (Blue Horse Press).

Lynne Bronstein is a poet, writer, and journalist. Her short stories and poetry have been published in *Lummox, Spectrum, Chiron Review, Playgirl, poeticdiversity, the Sisters in Crime anthology LAst resort,* and many other magazines. Her story "The Magic Candles"was read on National Public Radio. She has been nominated twice each for the Pushcart Prize and the Best of the Net Awards.

*

Ranney Campbell earned an MFA in fiction from the University of Missouri at St. Louis and lives in Southern California. Her poetry has been published by *Misfit Magazine, Shark Reef, Haight Ashbury Literary Journal* and others and her chapbook, *Pimp,* is published by Arroyo Seco Press.

*

Marne Carmean is a Los Angeles poet with poems published in *Plainsong* edited by Frank and Peggy Steele of Bowling Green, Kentucky. In 2012 The Bell Pepper field, was awarded $1,000.00 by the Green Heart Project, Final judge Kate Gale. A completed manuscript *Mexico Where Fences Bloom, Poems from this side and back,* currently being translated by Argentine poet Alicia Partnoy.

*

Eileen Carole is founder of the LA poetry group, The Writer's Corner and has published 17 anthologies with her label Pisces Publishing. Her anthologies are all centered on themes and the title inventory is growing; especially with the free time afforded by the Covid 19 Quarantine. ToWordsAndImages@Gmail.com

*

Patricia Carragon's latest chapbooks from Poets Wear Prada are *Meowku* (2019) and *The Cupcake Chronicles* (2017) and from Finishing Line Press, *Innocence* (2017). She hosts the Brooklyn-based Brownstone Poets and is the editor-in-chief of its annual anthology. Her debut novel, *Angel Fire,* is from Alien Buddha Press.

Neeli Cherkovski's body of poetry includes *Animal, Elegy for Bob Kaufman* and *Leaning Against Time,* for which he was awarded the 15th Annual PEN Oakland/Josephine Miles Literary Award in 2005. In 2017 he was awarded the Jack Mueller Poetry Prize by Lithic Press. Cherkovski also wrote biographies of Lawrence Ferlinghetti and Charles Bukowski.

*

John Dorsey is the author of several collections of poetry, including *The Prettiest Girl at the Dance* (Blue Horse Press, 2020) and *Which Way to the River: Selected Poems 2016-2020* (OAC Books, 2020). He was the winner of the 2019 Terri Award given out at the Poetry Rendezvous in Ashville, North Carolina.

*

Kim Dower has published four collections of poetry: *Air Kissing on Mars, Slice of Moon, Last Train to the Missing Planet,* and *Sunbathing on Tyrone Power's Grave.* Widely anthologized and nominated for five Pushcarts, she was City Poet Laureate of West Hollywood, from October 2016 to October 2018.

*

Carolina Rivera Escamilla was born in El Salvador and is a writer, actor, and documentarian. She lives in Los Angeles, CA. Her book of short stories, entitled *…after…* was published in 2015. Fellow of the Pen America Emerging Voices Program. www.carolinariveraescamilla.com

*

Consuelo G. Flores is a Poet, writer, memoirist, multi-media, installation artist, producer, director, performer, published author, arts administrator and promoter of cultural and community education and empowerment.

*

Los Angeles native **Amélie Frank**'s work has appeared in numerous regional, national, and international journals. She cofounded The Sacred Beverage Press and has served on the boards of the Valley Contemporary Poets and Beyond Baroque. Her biography appears in both *Who's Who in America* and *Who's Who of American Women.*

Texas-based writer and multi-genre artist **Tammy Melody Gomez** produced a short film ("TRASH: chauvin"); launched a virtual poetry series; contributed a poem published in *Together in a Sudden Strangeness* (Knopf); and was one of five female artists awarded the Texas Vignette grant. All of this happened during pandemic year 2020-2021.

*

Rachael Ikins is a 2016/18 Pushcart, 2013/18 CNY Book Award, 2018 Independent Book Award winner, & 2019 Vinnie Ream & Faulkner poetry finalist. She is author/illustrator of nine books in multiple genres. Her works have appeared in journals worldwide.

*

Victor D. Infante is a poet and journalist living in Worcester, Massachusetts, and the author of the book *City of Insomnia*, from Write Bloody Publishing.

*

Erika Jahneke is a writer, activist, and twitter geek based in Phoenix. She also writes the Bohemian Crip blog at bohemiancrip.blogspot.com, where she tries to wrangle with the disability experience in writing, pop culture and more.

*

Eleanor Kedney is the author of the full-length collection *Between the Earth and Sky* (C&R Press, 2020) and the chapbook *The Offering* (Liquid Light Press, 2016). Her work has appeared in a number of literary journals and anthologies. She lives in Tucson, AZ and Stonington, CT. Learn more at eleanorkedney.com.

*

Genevieve Legacy is a writer-artist living in WA State. With an MFA in Creative Writing from Lesley University, Legacy's poetry has been published in *The Hazmat Review, Napalm Health Spa, Poetry Superhighway, Sensitive Skin Magazine, Global Poemic* and on Writers.com.

Award-winning and widely published poet, author, journalist, and artivist **Aqueila M. Lewis-Ross** uses poetry as a catalyst for healing. Using her poetry collection, *Stop Hurting and Dance*, and performative workshop, "From a Victim to a Thriving Survivor: Learning How to Revive the Soul"; she honors what it means to live with resilience, love, and prosperity.

*

Peter Marti studied at Kerouac School of Disembodied Poetics. Member San Francisco based poetry collective Birthstone in the '70s, rock n roll singer in '80s, and part of *Wordland* performance poetry group in the '90s. Nominated for Pushcart Prize, 2002. Regularly published in print and on-line 'zines. Recent collections include: *Elephants I Didn't Ride, Thighbone Trumpet Echo*, and the upcoming *Son of Rocket Science.*

*

Jim McDonald has nearly a hundred acting credits on IMDB, and has written and performed his own work—plays, short films, stories, which have garnered numerous awards. His poetry and stories have been published in L.A. Writers and Poets Collective Journal: *Side-Eye on the Apocalypse, Blood and Bourbon* and *Satori Rebel.*

*

Richard Modiano is a native of Los Angeles. While a resident of New York City he became active in the literary community connected to the Poetry Project where he came to know Gregory Corso, Allen Ginsberg, Anne Waldman, William S. Burroughs and Ted Berrigan. From 2010 to 2019, he served as Executive Director of Beyond Baroque Literary/Arts Center where he produced and curated hundreds of literary events. In 2013 the Huffington Post named him one of the 200 people most responsible for keeping poetry vital in the US. Richard is a rank and file member of the Industrial Workers of the World. In 2019 he was elected Vice President of the California State Poetry Society.

Viggo Mortensen is an accomplished actor who doubles up as an author, poet, painter, musician, and photographer. Viggo established Perceval Press in 2002 to publish individuals who may otherwise have gone unnoticed and to do so without compromise.

*

Kendall Nelson is an educator and creative writer from Massachusetts who now resides in Los Angeles. She specializes in creative nonfiction and has presented research on translingual education and the value of storytelling as an educational method.

*

Marisela Norte is the author of *Peeping Tom Tom Girl*, a collection of poetry and prose. Her lates published work *In Memory of Frank O'Hara,* will be featured in an upcoming book about MOCA, the Museum of Contemporary Art. Norte's work featured in the MTA's *Out Your Window* project was recently named one of the best transit poems in the world by *The Atlantic Monthly.*

*

Suzanne O'Connell has two poetry collections published by Garden Oak Press: *A Prayer For Torn Stockings*, and *What Luck*. Find more of her work at: suzanneoconnell-poet.com

*

Marc Olmsted has appeared in *City Lights Journal, New Directions in Prose & Poetry, New York Quarterly, The Outlaw Bible of American Poetry* and a variety of small presses. He is the author of five collections of poetry, including *What Use Am I a Hungry Ghost?*, which has an introduction by Allen Ginsberg. Olmsted's 25-year relationship with Ginsberg is chronicled in his Beatdom Booms memoir *Don't Hesitate: Knowing Allen Ginsberg 1972-1997—Letters and Recollections,* available on Amazon.

Suzi Kaplan Olmsted has appeared in *The Sun, Maintenant, Blue Satellite, 51%, F.T.S., Big Scream, poetrysuperhighway.com, M.A.G., Lummox Journal, getunderground.com,* and *Napalm Health Spa.* She is also one of the illustrators of *The Ellyn Maybe Coloring Book* and the *Beatitude Golden Anniversary* volume. Nominated for a Pushcart Prize for a poem from her chapbook *Industrial Wallet* (Virgogray Press), she has another chapbook, *Elektra's Mouth,* also on Virgogray. Suzi lives in Portland, Oregon with her husband, poet Marc Olmsted, where they are slaves to the bidding of extraordinary cats Batty and Ellie.

*

Connie Owens Patton graduated from California State University, Stanislaus with a Bachelor of Arts in English. She has previously been published in African Voices. In 2020, her poem "Lie to Me" was featured on *Heard/Word Galleyway,* an on-line audio series.

*

Heather Pease's book of poetry is *Out of the Weeds.* Her poetry centers on mental health, feminism, self-acceptance, healing, and aims to make people think about subjects often stigmatized through society. Her work has appeared in various print anthologies and lit journals. She lives in Southern California.

*

Wang Ping is a poet, writer, installation artist and professor English Amerita. She has published 14 books of poetry, stories, and cultural studies. She's the founder of Kinship of Rivers project. www.kinshipofrivers.org. www.wangping.com.

*

Originally from the Pacific Northwest, **Kate Robinson** now contemplates the Atlantic from her home in Douarnenez, France, where she works as a translator and writes poetry.

Paula Rudnick is a former television writer/producer who has spent the last 30 years as a volunteer for non-profit organizations. She has been writing poetry since 2015. Her poems have been published in *Constellations* and *Truth Serum* anthologies, *Halfway Down the Stairs, Pilcrow & Dagger* and *The Jewish Journal.*

*

Norman Savage is the author of *Junk Sick: Confessions of an Uncontrolled Diabetic, MISTAH* and *Savage.* He passed away in October 2020.

*

Bryan Scheideck, an Oakland-based building contractor whose twenty-eight years of Buddhist practice include five spent working, studying, and traveling in Asia and twelve living at a Santa Cruz Mountain retreat center, relishes straddling urban life and rural. Poet Marc Olmsted notes, "Scheideck captures the non-theistic sacredness of the ordinary."

*

Mark States has authored three poetry collections, and has appeared in such publications as *Poetic Diversity, San Gabriel Valley Poetry Quarterly, Poetrymagazine.com, Muse Apprentice Guild* and *The November 3rd Club.* He is the former host of Poetry Express in Berkeley, California (2002-2011) and facilitator of Public Speaking for Poets workshops.

*

Laura Thurlow is a British-Canadian writer and filmmaker based in London. She is on Instagram @laurelbrae.

*

George Wallace is writer in residence at the Walt Whitman Birthplace, editor of Poetrybay, and author of 38 chapbooks of poetry. Based in the NYC performance scene, he travels internationally to share his work.

Julene Tripp Weaver, a native New Yorker, is a psychotherapist and writer in Seattle. Her book, *truth be bold—Serenading Life & Death in the Age of AIDS*, was a finalist for a Lambda Literary Award, and won the Bisexual Book Award. www.julenetrippweaver.com. Twitter: @trippweavepoet

*

Kurt Wit is a poet, playwright, and educator who currently resides in Los Angeles, CA. When he is not writing, speaking, teaching, or performing, Kurt also enjoys gardening, herbal tea and a good book.

*

Marc Zegans is the author of six collections of poems, most recently, *The Snow Dead* (CervenaBarva Press, 2020); two spoken word albums; several immersive theatrical productions including, *Sirens, Dreams and a Cat* (co-written with D. Lowell Wilder, 2020), and many short films. Explore his creative advisory services at mycreativedevelopment.com.

www.ingramcontent.com/pod-product-compliance
Lightning Source LLC
Chambersburg PA
CBHW042144160426
43201CB00022B/2408